RACING CARS

Written by

PENNY WORMS

FRANKLIN WATTS
LONDON • SYDNEY

This edition published in 2013 by
Franklin Watts
338 Euston Road
London NW1 3BH

Franklin Watts Australia
Level 17/207 Kent Street
Sydney NSW 2000

Series editor: Jeremy Smith
Design: Graham Rich
Cover design: Graham Rich
Picture research: Penny Worms

A CIP catalogue record for this book is available
from the British Library.

ISBN 978 1 4451 1891 8

Dewey classification: 629.2'28

The author would like to thank Felix Wills and the
following for their kind help and permission to use
images: Jeremy Davey from the Thrust team; Dave
Rowley from the Bloodhound team; and the media
teams at Audi, BMW and McLaren.

Picture Credits
Audi (UK): 7b, 15b, 16/17 (all images). BMW AG: 12/13.
Car Culture/Corbis: chapter page, 14/15, 19b. Carolyn
Kaster/AP/Press Association Images: 19t. Chris Wright,
www.bangerracing.com: 20/21 (all images). Getty Images:
18 (for NASCAR), 22. Jamie Duff/Press Association
Images: 13r. Jeremy Davey: 26l, 27r. Martin Rickett/PA
Wire/Press Association Images: 6/7. McLaren, www.
mclaren.com: title page, 8/9, 8b. PA/Press Association
Images: 14l. Shutterstock: 10/11 (all images), 23t,
23b, 25. Sutton/Press Association Images: 9b. www.
bloodhoundssc.com: 26/27. www.carphotolibrary.co.uk:
24t, 25b.

Every attempt has been made to clear copyright.
Should there be any inadvertent omission,
please apply to the publisher for rectification.

Printed in China

Franklin Watts is a division of Hachette Children's Books,
an Hachette UK company.
www.hachette.co.uk

Disclaimer: Some of the 'Stats and Facts' are
approximations. Others are correct at time of writing,
but will probably change.

CONTENTS

MOTOR RACING

Motor racing has been around for over 100 years. Since cars were invented, the makers and owners have wanted to see whose car is better or faster. Now motor racing is a worldwide sport, with people racing just about every kind of car.

SPEED

Some racing is all about speed. Cars built for drag racing and Formula One are designed to be fast, but it's not always the fastest that wins a race. It's the car that crosses the finish line first.

ENDURANCE

Some races are long and tough. Rally racing and long-distance races require cars that are built to overcome difficult challenges.

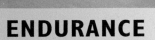

TEAMWORK

At the top level, motor racing is about serious sport and serious money. At the lowest level, it is mostly about fun. Usually there is a team involved, whether Audi professionals (left), or father and son. Often one person is the driver and the others build and maintain the vehicle. It's sport at its dirtiest, loudest and most exciting.

FORMULA ONE CAR

Formula One cars are the ultimate racing machines. Designed with only one seat for the driver, they are built using the most advanced **technology** and **engineering**. The teams spend millions of pounds trying to make their cars the fastest on the track.

The McLaren Mercedes MP4-24

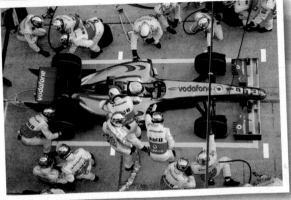

PIT STOP

Formula One cars are called open-wheel racers because their wheels are outside the main body of the car. This means they can be changed quickly in the **pits**.

- **Car:** General Formula One car
- **Top Speed:** up to 360 km/h (224 mph)
- **Race location:** Worldwide
- **Cost:** probably over £20 million (to build)
- **Claim to fame:** Formula One cars are the fastest around any race track.

AERODYNAMICS

The secret to a car's success depends on how well it slices through the air at high speed. Every feature of the car, from the wings to the driver's helmet, is designed to maximize **downforce** and reduce **drag**. Drag is caused by the movement of the air around the speeding car, which slows it down.

The front wing is designed to create downforce. This is the force caused by rushing air, forcing the front wheels down onto the track.

Scaled-down versions of the cars are built and tested in wind tunnels to check how **aerodynamic** they are.

KF-1 KART

Kart racing is one of the least expensive motor sports. It is open to anyone over eight years old (seven in the United States). Like Formula One cars, karts are single seater, open-wheel racers. KF1 is the top level, with the World Cup taking place in Japan every year.

PICK A CLASS

KF1 is just one class of kart racing. The classes are separated by the type of kart or track, age of driver or size of engine. The many classes ensure that the races are even, so they are a true test of the driver's skill.

FUTURE CHAMPIONS

The youngest drivers in KF1 races can be as young as 15 years old. Many Formula One and Nascar drivers started their careers racing karts, including Lewis Hamilton and Kimi Räikkönen.

STATS AND FACTS

- **Car:** General KF1 kart
- **Top Speed:** 140 km/h (85 mph)
- **Race location:** Worldwide
- **Cost:** approx £4,500 new
- **Claim to fame:** Jenson Button, 2009 Formula One World Champion, started out racing karts.

KF1

A KF1 kart has a 125**cc** engine. This number tells you how big the engine is. A small road car might have a 1200cc engine. This means that the kart's engine is far less powerful. However, a kart is much lighter than a car so it can reach high speeds more quickly.

WTCC RACER

Touring cars are road cars that have been specially adapted for racing on a track. The cars have the same bodies as cars you see on the road, but the engines are more powerful and the **mechanics** have been made strong enough for racing.

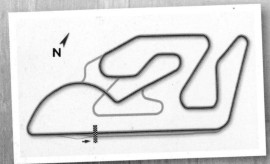

The track in Valencia, Spain.

WTCC TRACK

The cars that race in the World Touring Car Championship (WTCC) are usually **hatchbacks** or **saloons** with 2000cc engines. The racing tracks are circular but have bends and straights.

STATS AND FACTS

- **Car:** BMW 320si WTCC
- **Top Speed:** 245 km/h (152 mph)
- **Race location:** Worldwide
- **Cost:** £175,000
- **Claim to fame:** The most successful car in recent WTCC history.

WHEEL-TO-WHEEL COMBAT

What is exciting about touring car racing is that, beneath the stickers and spoilers, these are cars you see on the road. The difference on the track is that they are going at high speed, nudging one another and overtaking in wheel-to-wheel combat. To many fans, this is 'real' motor racing.

BMW

The BMW 320si (left) has been the most successful car in recent WTCC history, and touring car racing is BMW's most successful sport. The 320si road model (left) was developed alongside the racing model (opposite).

LE MANS RACER

In the late 1950s and early 1960s, Ferrari cars reigned supreme in motor racing. The Ferrari 250 Testarossa remains one of the most **iconic** racing cars of all time. Its design caused a stir when it first appeared because it was so beautiful and different from other sports cars around at the time.

24 HOURS OF LE MANS

Le Mans is one of the toughest, oldest car races in the world. The drivers race on the roads of Le Mans in France for an entire 24 hours (day and night). A Testarossa won it in 1958, 1960 and 1961. Back then, drivers had to run to their cars at the start.

TODAY'S LE MANS

Today's Le Mans cars are **prototypes** built specially for the race. In 2008, the Audi R10 TDI was the first diesel car to win. It used 41 litres of fuel per 100 km (Formula One cars use about 75 litres) and only needed 30 minutes in the pits over the entire 24 hours.

STATS AND FACTS

- **Car:** Ferrari 250 Testarossa
- **Top Speed:** 270 km/h (168 mph)
- **Race location:** France
- **Cost:** approx £60,000 in 1958/9
- **Claim to fame:** In 2009, a Testarossa sold for over £7.8 million, the highest price ever paid for a car.

FERRARI 250 TESTAROSSA

Fenders

According to one of the original car builders, the idea for the shape of the Testarossa was taken from the Formula One cars of the time. Ferrari introduced the rounded fenders to bring air in to the body to cool down the brakes.

GT RACER

The Audi R8 LMS is Audi's newest GT3 racer. GT stands for Gran Turismo and GT3 is the most recent category in the GT race series. GT3 cars are based on standard two-seater sports cars. The R8 LMS is an '**off-the-shelf**' racer, perfect for those who want to race, but Audi are producing road models, too.

Audi R8 LMS GT3

BRAND BUILDING

Many of the top sports car **brands** compete with Audi in the GT series, including Ferrari, Porsche, Lotus, BMW and Aston Martin. They develop their road cars in line with their racing cars, and success on the track raises a company's profile and makes its road cars more desirable.

STATS AND FACTS

- **Car:** Audi R8 LMS GT3
- **Top Speed:** over 322 km/h (200 mph)
- **Race location:** Europe
- **Cost:** approx £206,000 new
- **Claim to fame:** Based on the R8 Le Mans car which won the 24-hour race five times in 2001 to 2006.

SAFETY

A big concern when building any car is safety. It is even more important in racing cars because high-speed crashes are common. Racing cars have in-built **roll cages** and **cross bracing**. Both protect the driver if the car rolls over or crashes.

INSTANT GEAR SHIFTS

The R8 LMS has six gears and the driver changes gear by tapping a paddle on the steering wheel rather than using a gear stick. Low gears are used around corners. High gears are used along straights.

STOCK CAR

Stock car racing is the most popular form of racing in the United States. NASCAR is the ruling body and they decide how the cars should be built for each race series. The top series is the Sprint Cup and all cars must be American-made and built to a specific CoT design (Car of Tomorrow). This makes the races very competitive.

THE CAR OF TOMORROW

NASCAR changed the design for the Sprint Cup racers to make the cars slower, safer and cheaper to run. Because of the strict rules, each competitor is driving the same style of car with the same size engine. Winning is more about their racing ability rather than their car's performance.

STATS AND FACTS

- **Car:** General Sprint Cup stock car
- **Top Speed:** approx 301 km/h (187 mph)
- **Race location:** USA
- **Cost:** probably over £100,000 (to build)
- **Claim to fame:** In 2007, a new world stock car speed record was set at 244.9 mph (394 km/h).

MANUFACTURERS

The four cars currently built for the Sprint Cup are the Toyota Camry, the Ford Fusion, the Dodge Avenger and the Chevrolet Impala. The CoT models closely resemble the road-going **production cars.**

SIDE-TO-SIDE COMBAT

With over 40 cars on the **starting grid**, side-to-side contact is common. The cars are built with rails, bars and steel plating on the driver's side. They also have special foam pads inside the doors that absorb the energy of an impact, like a punch bag.

BANGER

Banger racing usually takes place on short oval dirt tracks. Like other car races, the first car to finish wins. The difference is that banger drivers stop at nothing to get there. They push their own cars beyond their limit and try to get competitor's cars off the track. Wrecks are common!

RACE TO THE END

At a banger meeting, there are different types of race. Some are non-contact. Others are team races with two or four cars chained together. Often there is a Demolition Derby at the end. This is not really a race. The winner is the last car moving, having demolished the other cars.

SAFETY FIRST

The most important part of any banger is its roll cage. The cars often end up on their sides or upside down. There are no rules governing banger racing, so each driver needs to make sure they are fully protected.

STATS AND FACTS

- **Car:** General banger
- **Top Speed:** up to 100 km/h (60 mph) on a clear track
- **Race location:** Worldwide
- **Cost:** probably no more than £400
- **Claim to fame:** There are more crashes in banger racing than any other motor sport.

BEST BANGERS

Bangers are often pieced together using spare parts from scrap cars. Small hatchbacks are the most common form of banger but it is often hard to tell what the original car was under all the paint, plating and dents.

DRAGSTER

Drag racing is the loudest motorsport on earth. Two cars race in a straight line over a set distance, usually 400 metres (a quarter of a mile). The first over the finish line wins. The fastest are the top-fuel dragsters. They go so fast they need parachutes to slow them down. The world record over 400 metres is 4.428 seconds.

ROCKET FUEL

The top-fuel dragsters run on a blend of fuel that is similar to rocket fuel. No wonder the cars can go almost as fast as jet planes. Racing top-fuel dragsters is also very dangerous!

STATS AND FACTS

- **Car:** General top-fuel dragster
- **Top Speed:** 540.98 km/h (336.15 mph)
- **Race location:** Worldwide
- **Cost:** £150,000 approx
- **Claim to fame:** The sound of top-fuel drag racing can be heard over 13km (8 miles) away.

STICKY TYRES

Before any drag race, the tyres are heated up by what is called 'a burnout'. Water is sprayed onto the wheels and the driver presses the **throttle** hard for three seconds. The wheels spin, which heats up the rubber to make them sticky. This helps them to grip the track for a fast start.

FUNNY CARS

The other classes of drag racing include the Funny Car. These dragsters look a little like normal road cars but underneath they are turbo-charged speedsters!

RALLY CAR

Rally racing is the cross-country of motor sport. Races are on public and private roads or tracks, so rally cars need to be built for both. The Ford Focus RS is based on the production car but has been heavily adapted for this type of racing.

ALL CHANGE

The World Rally Championship is top-class rallying. It takes place over three days and on different courses. Some courses are snow and ice. Some are roads or gravel tracks. The car's **suspension** needs adapting for each race. A car's suspension connects a car to its wheels. It has **shock absorbers** and springs for a smooth ride and softer landings.

TURBO-CHARGED

The Ford Focus RS rally car is specially built to cope with the tough courses. It is four-wheel drive, meaning the engine drives all four wheels. Also, its engine is turbo-charged to give it more **acceleration** and speed.

STATS AND FACTS

- **Car:** Ford Focus RS
- **Top Speed:** 259 km/h (161 mph)
- **Race location:** Europe, Australia and South America
- **Cost:** £25,000+ (road car price)
- **Claim to fame:** In 2008, Jari-Matti Latvala (22) was the youngest driver to win a world rally in a Ford Focus RS.

FROM TRACK TO ROAD

Ford, like other car makers, race cars to learn lessons about performance and safety. They apply what they learn to their road cars.

LAND SPEED CAR

In 1997, Thrust SSC broke the land speed record with a top speed of 1227.985 km/h (763.035 mph). It is officially the first car to travel faster than the speed of sound. Now the race is on to beat the record with Bloodhound SSC, the latest project from the Thrust team.

THRUST SSC

The world record was set in the Black Rock Desert in the USA. It is a dry lake bed and extremely wide and flat. Very few places on earth offer such a soft, smooth racing surface.

Thrust SSC

THE SPEED OF SOUND

The speed of sound is the speed at which sound travels through the air (appox 1200 km/h). When there is a loud noise in the distance, such as a car horn or an explosion, you don't hear it the instant it happens. It takes a little time for the sound to travel to your ears. So, Thrust was actually travelling faster than the noise it was making!

STATS AND FACTS

- **Car:** Thrust SSC
- **Top Speed:** 1227.985 km/h (763.035 mph)
- **Race location:** USA
- **Cost:** Thought to be approx £4 million
- **Claim to fame:** Officially, the first supersonic car.

BLOODHOUND SSC

With Bloodhound SSC (Super Sonic Car), the aim is to reach a speed of 1609 km/h (1000 mph) while controlling the car and keeping all four wheels on the ground.

Bloodhound SSC

At full speed Bloodhound will cover 4½ football pitchs per second!

Thrust SSC was powered by two jet engines. Bloodhound SSC will use one jet engine to get to 563 km/h (350 mph), then a rocket to blast it to 1609 km/h (1000 mph).

GLOSSARY

aerodynamic designed to travel through air easily at speed

acceleration the rate at which a car builds up speed

brands what makes one type of car or product different and distinctive from another

cc cubic centimetres, the size of a car's engine

cross bracing metal bars that go across the roll cage to make it even stronger

downforce the force caused by air rushing over a moving car that pushes it down onto a track or road

drag air movement around a moving car that pulls on the car and slows it down

engineering the use of science in designing and building engines

fenders guards over each wheel of a car

hatchbacks cars that have a lift-up door at the back

iconic something that, over time, has become an icon or symbol

mechanics the moving parts of a car. Also the name for people who fix cars

off-the-shelf something that can be used as soon as it is bought and does not have to be changed or adapted in any way

pits the place on a race track where cars make quick stops for fuel or tyre changes

production cars cars that are made in a factory and go on general sale

prototype a product made and used for testing before others are made, to see if it works and how it can be improved

roll cage a strong, metal frame built into a car that protects the driver if it crashes and rolls over

saloons family sized cars with two or four doors and a boot

shock absorbers air or oil-filled car parts that soak up bumps in the road

starting grid the position of the cars at the start of a race

suspension a system of springs and shock absorbers that work between the body of a car and its wheels

technology the use of science and the latest equipment

throttle the pedal that is pressed to release fuel into the engine to make the car go faster. Also known as an accelerator

INDEX